Chicken Soup for the Soul®
Cartoons for Dads

CHICKEN SOUP FOR THE SOUL® CARTOONS FOR DADS

Jack Canfield
Mark Victor Hansen
John McPherson
Creator of *Close to Home*

Health Communications, Inc.
Deerfield Beach, Florida

www.hcibooks.com
www.chickensoup.com

Library of Congress Cataloging-in-Publication Data

McPherson, John, date.
Chicken soup for the soul : cartoons for dads / [compiled by] Jack Canfield, Mark Victor Hansen ; [cartoons by] John McPherson.
p. cm.
ISBN 0-7573-0089-8 (TP)
1. Fatherhood—Caricatures and cartoons. 2. Fathers—Caricatures and cartoons. 3. American wit and humor, Pictorial. I. Canfield, Jack, date. II. Hansen, Mark Victor. III. Title.

NC1429.M275A4 2003a
741.5'973—dc22

2003060071

ISBN 0-7573-0089-8

Publisher: Health Communications, Inc.
3201 S.W. 15th Street
Deerfield Beach, Florida 33442-8190

R-10-03

Cover design by Larissa Hise Henoch
Inside formatting by Lawna Patterson Oldfield

With love, for all dads everywhere.

—Jack Canfield and Mark Victor Hansen

For Dad, thanks for all your laughter.

—John McPherson

Other books by John McPherson

Chicken Soup for the Soul® Cartoons for Moms

Close to Home

Dangerously Close to Home

One Step Closer to Home

The Silence of the Lamberts

Close to Home Revisited

Home: The Final Frontier

Close to Home Unplugged

Striking Close to Home

The Close to Home Survival Guide

The Get Well Book

High School Isn't Pretty

Close to Home Uncut

The Scourge of Vinyl Car Seats

Close to Home Exposed

The Honeymoon Is Over

Acknowledgments

We wish to express our heartfelt gratitude to the following people who helped make this book possible:

Our publisher, Peter Vegso, for his vision and commitment to bringing *Chicken Soup for the Soul* to the world.

Patty Aubery, for being there on every step of the journey with love, laughter and endless creativity.

Kathy Brennan-Thompson, for spearheading this project throughout the various phases of its completion.

Nancy Autio and Barbara LoMonaco, for helping with the final selection of cartoons.

Maria Nickless and Stephanie Thatcher, for their enthusiastic marketing, public relations support and brilliant sense of direction.

Patty Hansen, for her thorough and competent handling of the legal and licensing aspects of the *Chicken Soup for the Soul* books. You are magnificent at the challenge!

Laurie Hartman, for being a precious guardian of the *Chicken Soup* brand.

Erick Baldwin, for his dedicated service in helping to create this book.

Jack and Mark's wonderful staff, who support their businesses with skill and love. Thanks to Dana Drobny, Teresa Esparza, Leslie Riskin, Veronica Romero, Robin Yerian, Heather McNamara, Tasha Boucher, D'ette Corona, Russ Kamalski, Jesse Ianniello, Jody Emme, Trudy Marschall, Michelle Adams, Dee Dee Romanello, Shanna Vieyra, Lisa Williams, Gina Romanello, Brittany Shaw, Dena Jacobson, Tanya Jones, Mary McKay and David Coleman.

Lisa Drucker and Susan Heim, our editors at Health Communications, Inc., for their devotion to excellence.

Terry Burke and the marketing and public-relations departments at Health Communications, Inc., for doing such an incredible job supporting our books.

The art department at Health Communications, Inc., for their talent, creativity and unrelenting patience in producing book covers and inside designs that capture the essence of *Chicken Soup*: Larissa Hise Henoch, Lawna Patterson Oldfield, Andrea Perrine Brower, Lisa Camp, Anthony Clausi and Dawn Von Strolley Grove.

Thank you to all of the *Chicken Soup for the Soul* coauthors, who make it so much of a joy to be part of this *Chicken Soup* family.

To Greg Melvin, Lee Salem, Denise Clark, Sadie Webb and the other great folks at Universal Press Syndicate for their ongoing support of John and his work.

Special thanks to John Vivona and the Universal Press sales force for their hard work on John's behalf. You guys are the best.

Lastly, thanks to Chris Millis, John's right-hand man.

We are truly grateful and love you all!

Introduction

Throughout history, fathers have been looked to for strength, support and security. More than ever in today's turbulent and ever-changing world, we continue to reach out to our fathers as anchors.

The role of the father in the family structure is important and unique. Fathers are called upon to be husbands, providers, teachers and disciplinarians. They often manage to do all this while also acting as role models and friends to their children.

With this collection of cartoons, we seek to pay a humorous tribute to dads and the many roles they play, from supporting moms through pregnancy and birth, changing diapers and playing catch to teaching teenagers to drive. Dads take the kids fishing, build tree houses, seem to never ask for directions, interrogate their daughters' boyfriends and have heard every excuse in the book. They tuck the kids in at night and act as storytellers. Fathers wear many hats.

We hope these cartoons make you laugh and that you see a bit of your own father, or even yourself, in them. Most importantly, may these cartoons cause you to recognize the many roles and responsibilities inherent in the role of the father and remind you to appreciate the unique men who are lucky enough to be called "Dad."

PARENTHOOD SIMULATOR
ON
OFF
TURBO
SETTING
2 A.M. FEEDING
LOST PACIFIER
CHICKEN POX
WET BED
TERRIBLE TWOS
COLICKY BABY
COLICKY TRIPLETS
PROJECTILE VOMITING
UNSOLICITED ADVICE
McPHERSON

"Yeah, I know your contractions are only two minutes apart. But if you can just hang in there until tomorrow, I'll win the baby pool at work."

★ THE MAN OF THE '90S GUIDE TO FATHERHOOD ★
CHAP. 1. YOU CAN STILL DO EVERYTHING YOU USED TO DO.
CHAP. 2. HOW TO CHANGE A DIAPER ON THE GOLF COURS
CHAP. 3. BOWLING WITH A BABY IN ONE ARM MAY ACTUALLY IMPROVE YOUR SCORE.
CHAP. 4. PROOF THAT LATE-NIGHT POKER GAMES HELP STIMULATE A BABY'S LANGUAGE SKILLS.
CHAP. 5. TENNIS: DON'T LET THAT BABY ON YOUR BACK HAMPER YOUR NET GAME
McPHERSON

Cleaning your house while your kids are still growing up is like shoveling the walk before it stops snowing.

Phyllis Diller

To avoid disturbing the kids' elaborate toy layouts,
the Nortsteins wisely installed a zip-line in the family room.

THAT'S IT, HONEY. BREATHE OUT SLOWLY. GOOD. TRY TO RELAX. OK, WAIT FOR THE NEXT CONTRACTION...
McPHERSON

NO THROWING FOOD, EVER!
THE WONDERS OF IN UTERO DISCIPLINE
McPHERSON

The place of the father in a modern suburban family is a very small one, particularly if he plays golf.

Bertrand Russell

WHAT YOU SHOULD BE DOING TODAY!
* PAID FOR BY THE WIVES OF THE TOWN OF SHENKSVILLE.
3
McPHERSON

"Kevin, if you don't say the blessing, you're going to make God very, very angry."

Thanks to the wonders of virtual reality, fathers can now completely experience the miracle of giving birth.

The most important thing a father can do for his children is to love their mother.

Theodore Hesburgh

With the kids' spelling skills rapidly improving, the Colemans devised another way to communicate during dinner.

The growing interest in health and fitness has had an effect on even the longest-standing traditions.

OK, THE NORTH STAR IS OVER THERE...
FOR CRYIN' OUT LOUD! WILL YOU JUST PULL OVER AND ASK SOMEONE WHERE ROUTE 17 IS?!
McPHERSON

"I've been telling him for years to get up and get some exercise. Now he's actually begun to morph into the cellular structure of the couch."

"What? Oh, geez, no. The baby's not due until September. We just got our sonogram results today."

Tiger Woods: the early months.

"It's the latest version of the stress test.
We'll monitor your heart rate as you try to
feed these seven hungry babies with just one bottle."

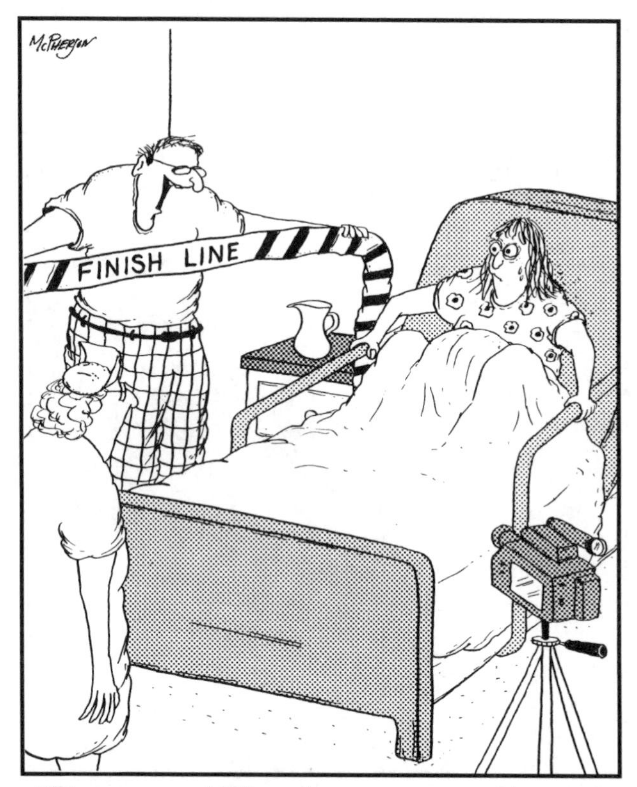

"Oh, come on! Where's your sense of humor? Just let me tape it to your knees and get some video footage while the midwife is delivering the baby."

". . . So, while you were sleeping, I talked to the doctors and they worked it out so you can still keep building the deck when you get home."

You will always be your child's favorite toy.

Vicki Lansky

"Wow! That was neat, Dad!
Okay, teach me how to throw it! Dad?!"

"So, is this your first baby?"

Knowing that many men resist going to the doctor, Hartman Medical Center built a new facade for its entryway.

MATERNITY
McPHERSON

MASTER
LAMAZE
IN JUST
10 MINUTES
McPHERSON

McPherson
POWER FLEX

"I'm sorry, folks, but the name you chose for your baby, Zebulon Euphrates Miller, was rejected by our nerd-checking software."

Unable to bear the humiliation of having her geeky dad drop her off at school, Amanda insisted that he dress as a rock star.

“Geesh! Check out the mug on that poor little devil!”

Using computer imaging, Dr. Wahlig was able to show parents how their child would look in fifteen years if they decided not to get him braces.

"Sorry, folks. Insurance regulations.
After the baby is born, you've got one hour to
recover and then out you go!"

MATERNITY
WHAT WILL YOUR CHILD BE LIKE?
CALL THE PSYCHIC INFANT HOTLINE
* JUST $4.95/MINUTE
McPherson

TODAY'S
HIGH
9.6
LOW
1.2
MEASURE YOUR BABY'S CUTENESS LEVEL WITH
CUTE-A-SCOPE!
ONLY $5!
8.7
CUTE
-A-
SCOPE

*Parenthood is a lot easier
to get into than out of.*

Bruce Lansky

"He's 2 1/2 days old and he's already had nine time-outs!"

A lot of parents pack up their troubles
and send them off to summer camp.

Raymond Duncan

It was not until they entered the principal's office that the Keppelmans realized the severity of Ryan's discipline problem.

"Hey, you want him to sleep through the night, don't you?"

"I, Jimmy Delmonte, do solemnly swear that the feeding, walking and overall care of Sparkles shall be my responsibility and mine alone. . . ."

"They pride themselves on being tough on discipline around here."

Though made of simply a crate and a harmless old lawnmower engine, the mere sound of the Spankomatic assured that it never had to be used.

The one thing children wear out faster than shoes is parents.

John J. Plomp

"Are you gonna make me return the chemistry set?"

For one fleeting instant, while all the other adults weren't looking, Dave watched dumbstruck as every baby in the maternity ward did the Wave.

"Uh, yeah, Homework Help Line? I need to have you explain the quadratic equation in roughly the amount of time it takes to get a cup of coffee."

Most of us become parents long before we have stopped being children.

Mignon McLaughlin

"Come on! Where's your sense of humor?
All I'm going to do is stroll her through the mall!"

The downside of wearing diapers to the beach.

"Every diaper has a lottery ticket on it. In the last five weeks, Jim's won $40 and I haven't changed a single diaper."

My father didn't tell me how to live; he lived,
and let me watch him do it.

Clarence Budington Kelland

The '90s dad: able to spend time with his kids while still indulging in his favorite sport.

"Let's put it on high for twenty minutes.
She's gotta fall asleep after that."

SKIP, the baby is Finally asleep! Turn the car off now, coast into the driveway and crawl in through the basement window.
McPHERSON

McPHERSON
HELP! WE ARE LOST BUT OUR DAD WON'T STOP TO ASK DIRECTIONS!

DIAPERS
FOR BOYS 22-24 lbs. WHO CRAWL
★unscented
★Train design on waistband
DIAPERS
FOR GIRLS 17-19 lbs. WHO STAND UP BUT DON'T WALK.
★orange scent
★doll design
DIAPERS
FOR GIRLS 29-30 lbs. WHO RIDE TRIKES
★unscented
★Regis+Kathy Lee design
DIAPERS
FOR BOYS 25-27 lbs. WHO JUMP UP AND DOWN AND YELL
★peach scent
★car design
DIAPERS
FOR BOYS 31-32 lbs. WHO WRESTLE WITH DAD A LOT
★musk scent
DIAPERS
FOR BOYS 8-9 lbs. WHO WIGGLE AROUND A LOT
★basil scent
★David Letterman design
DIAPERS
FOR GIRLS 33 lbs. WHO SHOULD BE POTTY-TRAINED BUT AREN'T
★pine scent
★cow design
M.PETERSON

The dream appliance for new parents.

“Will you relax?! They told us to look after the kids while they went to the craft fair. So we’re looking after the kids, right?”

People who say they sleep like a baby usually don't have one.

Leo J. Burke

"Ha! There! You see?!!
My eyes are TWICE as bloodshot as yours!
It's YOUR turn to get up with the baby!"

The Thackleys couldn't help but be jealous of the Furmans' new all-terrain stroller.

"Total cost of the Wagners' RV: $62,195.
Total cost of our RV: $932.41!"

Through well-planned provocation, Vince was able to harvest enough toilet paper during Halloween to keep the family supplied for an entire year.

"Ooooh, look! *Nice* lawn mower! Lawn mower is our *friend!* Hey, there's Mr. Snow Shovel! *Good* Mr. Snow Shovel! Let's hang your new friend right above your crib!"

McPherson
RUMBLE!
WUMP
CLANK!

"I knew you would like it."

"Okay, everyone. Very funny. Vulture-shaped Mylar balloons to circle my head. Ha, ha, ha."

"And remember, I'm not just the Nose Hair Club president, I'm also a client."

After four hours of lugging a twenty-eight-pound toddler around a mall, Doug is stricken by a case of Baby-Backpack Syndrome.

"Are you insane?! When I said I smelled an odor, I meant you should change his diaper, not slap one of those deodorizing discs on him!"

*If your kids are giving you a headache,
follow the directions on the aspirin bottle,
especially the part that says
"keep away from children."*

Susan Savannah

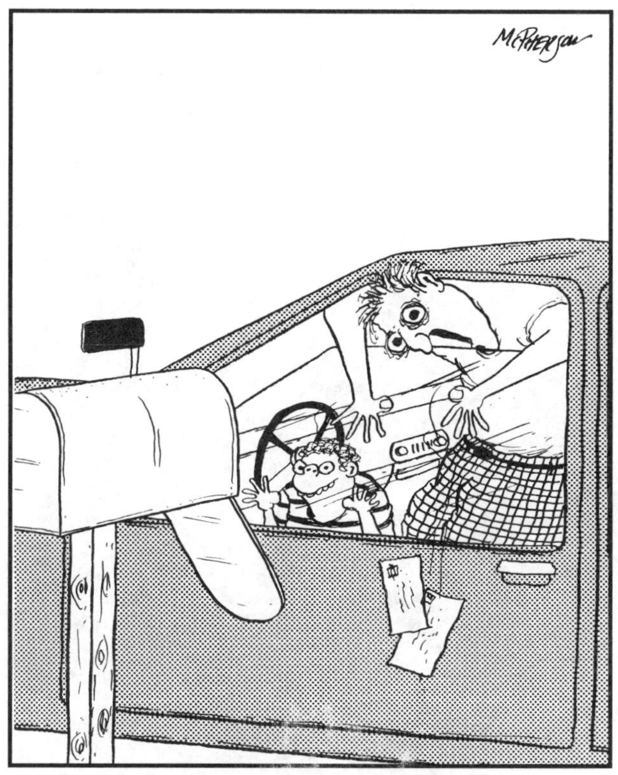

"Okay, Tommy! Fun time's over!
Push the button to lower the window!
Tommy! Push the button!"

Getting a whiff of the dirty diaper, Jerry quickly kicks into diaper duty avoidance mode.

An essential parenting skill: speeding up bedtime by condensing children's books.

"Here it is! Glerf! It means 'Oprah's on'!"

"Yeah, I know she shouldn't play with her food. But that's pretty good!"

"When you take into account rest stops for me, Louise and the kids, I figure that towing the porta-john will save us about fifty minutes a day."

Having spotted the approaching IRS agent,
Rodney hurried the family into the tax shelter.

"So den, weez tie on t'ree cinderblocks, and . . . BADA-BING! . . . Down to da bottom he goes! And dat was da last time anybody saw Bennie Da Mole!"

Another gullible parent is sucked in by pharmaceutical quackery.

"The manual says it needs 187 'D' batteries."

Frantically dialing Tom's cell phone number,
Cindy's worst fears are confirmed.

Insanity is hereditary—you get it from your kids.

Sam Levenson

"He's got Raffi-itis, Mrs. Fernweld.
There are seven kids' songs stuck in his head
that we'll try to blast out using some Jimi Hendrix tunes."

Blessed indeed is the man who hears
many gentle voices call him father!

Lydia M. Child

After the seventh consecutive viewing of *Barney Goes to Cleveland,* Alan suffers a spontaneous boredom attack.

"Well, Mr. McGraw, I understand you have a paper cut.
Let's take a look."

"Watch your step. There's quite a drop-off over here."

The Ridleys devise a way to prepare themselves for summer weekends at the shore.

"G'day, mate! First time to Australia?"

Prior to visiting Orlando, the La Clairs had wisely purchased a copy of "The Blueprints of Disney's Utility Tunnels."

"For an additional one dollar per ticket, would you like to buy disability insurance?"

Don't worry that children never listen to you;
worry that they are always watching you.

Robert Fulghum

"Wow! I haven't heard Dad scream that loud since we carved our names into the hood of his Corvette!"

For an additional $100 per person, Disney World now offers Go-to-the-Head-of-the-Line cards.

A typical group photo taken with an auto-timer.

"Okay, let's have one more shot.
This time, try not to look directly at the flash."

WELCOME TO KENSINGTON ZOO
ANIMALS THAT WILL SCARE YOUR KIDS
ANIMALS THAT SLEEP ALL THE TIME
ANIMALS WHOSE ODORS WILL MAKE YOU GAG
ANIMALS THAT SCRATCH THEMSELVES IN EMBARRASSING PLACES
McPHERSON

"And here's a feature I *know* you're going to love! It's got a built-in audio sensor that sends a mild electric jolt to the back seat anytime it detects the phrase, 'Are we there yet?'"

Bizarre though it was, the Merkles had stumbled onto a system for picking stocks that netted them $11,761 in just five months.

Mother Nature, in her infinite wisdom, has instilled within each of us a powerful biological instinct to reproduce; this is her way of assuring that the human race, come what may, will never have any disposable income.

Dave Barry

SNEAKER WORLD
4% A.P.R. FINANCING AVAILABLE ON ALL SNEAKERS!
McPHERSON

"Okay, Captain Anxiety. I took some Polaroids before we left. Exhibit A: the stove with all burners clearly in the 'off' position. Exhibit B: the back door with its deadbolt latched. Exhibit C: my curling iron unplugged . . ."

Without a doubt, one of the all-time
worst places to get a flat.

"Oh, I forgot to tell you. I let the kids take the spare tire to play with in the sandbox."

"Polaroid No. I: Ming's Chinese Laundry. Polaroid 2:45 minutes later, same laundry. Oh, look! What's that ahead? It's . . . Ming's Chinese Laundry! *Now* do you believe we're driving in circles?!"

McPherson
TUES. 8 p.m. FIRST MONTHLY SUPPORT GROUP "MEN WHO HATE TO STOP AND ASK FOR DIRECTIONS"

"Boy, that's a shame. Pouring rain when you wanted to play more golf. Well, seems like a good opportunity to paint the living room."

"It's got a sensor on it that homes in on the smell of aftershave anytime the grass gets to be three inches high."

AND THEN THE MEAN MOMMY TOOK THE KIND DADDY'S GOLF CLUBS AND BROKE THEM ALL IN HALF. "CLEAN THE GARAGE!" SHE ROARED, AS SMOKE POURED FROM HER NOSTRILS.
FRANK!
McPHERSON

"Hey, the sooner he learns to crawl, the sooner he'll learn to walk. The sooner he learns to walk, the sooner he can mow the lawn."

"Oh, look at that! First a lawn mower and now a snow shovel!
How about a big thank you for your father, Marty?!"

As a child my family's menu consisted of two choices: take it, or leave it.

Buddy Hackett

After months of gathering dust, the Norsteens' $1,500 treadmill is finally put to use.

Children are a great comfort in your old age—
and they help you reach it faster, too.

Lionel Kauffman

Life in the home office.

Raising kids is part joy and part guerilla warfare.

Ed Asner

"Well, technically visiting hours are over, but I don't see the harm in giving you another hour."

"How many times do I have to tell you not to slam the door?! When your father comes in from shoveling, he's going to have something to say about this!"

Bud Wellman discovers the true value of
a self-propelled lawn mower.

". . . then, you just turn the crank, and . . . VOILÀ!"

Using stimulus/response, the Nelsons hoped to discourage Jeremy from engaging in dangerous activities as a teenager.

Always end the name of your child with a vowel,
so that when you yell, the name will carry.

Bill Cosby

"What are the chances I could get
a $7,000 advance on my allowance?"

"Sorry, Dad. We got a little carried away with the snowman-building."

"Now don't be upset with the kids, Ray.
They only did it so you'd be able to drive in the car-pool lane."

Children are unpredictable.
You never know what inconsistency they're going to catch you in next.

Franklin P. Jones

"Okay, that's enough! I paid $300 for that PlayStation! You kids darn well better get in here and play with it!"

A three-year-old child is a being who gets almost as much fun out of a fifty-six-dollar set of swings as it does out of finding a small green worm.

Bill Vaughan

"Well, hon, it took $1,400 and fifty-seven hours of hard labor, but we did it! I can't wait to see the looks on the kids' faces!"

"I don't think you need to push quite so hard, Dad."

"Ed rents it for the entire NFL season."

Parents at the Millview eight- to ten-year-old soccer league were much calmer since the installation of the hot tubs.

"My husband said to send the bill to the New York Jets."

The quickest way for a parent to get a child's attention is to sit down and look comfortable.

Lane Olinghouse

"For crying out loud! Can't you take a hint?!
Get outside and play ball with your son!"

Little League officials soon got wise to Jason's dad and the remote-control glove.

By tapping into the stabilizing power
of gyroscopes, Wade was able to teach
his son to walk at just five months.

"Do me a favor and act like there's nothing wrong with it.
My dad's pretty proud of the fact that he
put it together all by himself."

Ray hoped that the stroller would put an end to strangers referring to Jason as a "cute little girl."

To encourage fathers to take on more child-care responsibilities, Pampers comes out with its new line of sports-trivia diapers.

"That goofball over there offered me five bucks to put this helmet on his kid long enough to get a photo."

GERTSVILLE
LITTLE LEAGUE
1 2 3 4 5
R H E
WHALES 7 11 5 10
33 37 27
GRACKLES 14 6 12
32 21 31
ACTION PHOTOS OF YOUR LITTLE LEAGUER TAKEN AND RETOUCHED TO LOOK LIKE HE *ACTUALLY CAUGHT THE BALL!!*
$20
VISA
BEFORE
AFTER
CLICK!
McPHERSON

"For the 100th time, I'm sorry I bent your new driver while trying to unclog the toilet!"

"Will you shut up about how great the fishing is?!"

"Say good-bye to our fly problem!"

If you wonder where your child left his roller skates,
try walking around the house in the dark.

Leopold Fechtner

"It was the cutest thing!
Jordan felt so bad about leaving his marbles on the stairs,
he made this cast for his dad out of Legos!"

"Will you two knock it off with the train sound effects?!"

"Try jiggling the handle."

"Mikey, turn off Road Runner and try to help Daddy! Tell Daddy what buttons to push to fix a general fault protection error/hard drive failure!"

"When I was a kid, we had to get up, walk clear across the room, and turn a dial on the TV whenever we wanted to change the channel."

When my kids become wild and unruly,
I use a nice, safe playpen. When they're finished, I climb out.

Erma Bombeck

"Okay, now!"

A baby has a way of making a man out of his father and a boy out of his grandfather.

Angie Papadakis

"Wow! First a drum and now cymbals!
Thanks, Grandma and Grandpa!"

"You got any bright ideas how to get a peanut butter and jelly sandwich out of the VCR?"

"Well, Tim, I thought that while you were waiting for Diane to get ready, you'd like to hear some of my hot new tunes."

Labor Day is a glorious holiday because your child will be going back to school the next day. It would have been called Independence Day, but that name was already taken.

Bill Dodds

To help them stave off empty-nest syndrome in later years, the Martinos made a point of recording every unpleasant parenting experience.

The habit of wearing one's cap backward actually began with Davy Crockett's son, Brian.

"Don't worry, it's not a real tattoo.
I just want to see the look on Dad's face
when he brings his boss home for tonight's big dinner."

"Wooo! Awesome! 187 rolls of duct tape!
Tell me this baby won't pass inspection NOW!"

"My seventeen-year-old drove the car into the garage door three times, so I finally just said the heck with it and installed the beads."

Heredity is what sets the parents
of a teenager wondering about each other.

Laurence J. Peter

"This'll be a good chance to test
that rust-proofing job on the car, huh, Dad?"

Never lend your car to anyone to whom you have given birth.

Erma Bombeck

"Now, here's the funny part, Dad."

Using technology to allay your child's fears.

"Relax! This is just until the tax assessor comes here tomorrow."

"Help me play a little prank on my husband. Start walking away with these while exclaiming that you can't believe you bought a set of new graphite clubs for ten bucks."

McPHERSON
CLEEBER ORTHODONTICS
LOAN DEPARTMENT
NOW AVAILABLE:
20-YEAR 8.5% APR

Ask your child what he wants for dinner only if he's buying.

Fran Lebowitz

"Okay, let's see . . . peas, meatloaf, potatoes and milk. We'll say $3.50. Oh, wait, you had seconds, didn't you, Brad?"

"Adding you to our car insurance as a teenager will triple our rate.
From now on, wear this mask and overcoat,
and go by the name 'Uncle Mort.'"

"I hope this is just some kind of cruel joke, Dad!"

"Oh, I forgot to tell you. Your father just installed a security system to warn him anytime somebody sets the temperature above sixty-five degrees."

"Oh, you mean this? My dad's on this big kick lately about making sure we turn out lights when we leave a room."

"Darn it all, Melissa! Take it easy on the toilet paper!
Ya think they just GIVE that stuff away?!"

By soaking the telephone in pure bear musk, Carl was able to reduce the family's phone bill by 83 percent.

"You'll get your $50 deposit back
as long as you bring Darlene home by midnight."

"Well, I'll be! Sheila, it's *another* electronic listening device! Santa's helpers must have bugged our house to see who's being naughty or nice!"

By the time a man realizes that maybe his father was right,
he usually has a son who thinks he's wrong.

Charles Wadworth

“Now’s the part where you’re supposed to say, ‘The important thing is that you’re okay, son.’ Give it a try, Dad. Eight simple words.”

"Sorry about this, Barb and Ted.
It's just until the kids get through college."

McPHERSON
TROMP! TROMP! TROMP!
JING! JING! JING!
CLICK!
HOOF-MATIC!
★ THRILL YOUR KIDS WITH THE SOUND OF REINDEER ON THE ROOF!

When the going gets tough, switch to power tools.

The Red Green Show, *PBS*

Bill finds an innovative way to put the lights on the tree.

Using time-lapse photography, Doug Sparling proves that a perfectly coiled strand of Christmas lights will tangle itself in the course of a year.

The Nargleys perform their post-holiday ritual
of trying to blow all the needles off the tree in one breath.

Likely as not, the child you can do the least with will do the most to make you proud.

Mignon McLaughlin

"Mind? Are you kidding?
Dad's gonna *love* being able to get the mail
while he's still in his underwear!"

To bring up a child in the way he should go,
travel that way yourself once in a while.

Josh Billings

At the Sheboygan, Wis., No-Hands-Allowed Snow Shoveling Contest.

By the time he turned thirteen, Bryan was starting to see through his father's little scam.

"Well, when you get your grades up to a B average, THEN you can choose your own wallpaper."

"Hey, Dad. I heard an interesting story. Did you know that Einstein failed math?! Really, it's true! Pretty amazing, hugh, Dad?! Smart guy like Einstein doing crummy at math."

A curfew was not something to be taken lightly in the Anderson household.

"This? Oh, nothing. It's just a radio-transmitter collar so Lisa's dad can track you down if you don't get her home by midnight. No big deal."

"It's very simple, Diane. When you leave on a date, you punch out on the time clock. When you get home, you punch in."

It is amazing how quickly the kids can learn to drive a car, yet are unable to understand the lawnmower, snowblower or vacuum cleaner.

Ben Bergor

"And here are the keys to the car."

"Sorry about this, Mark.
My dad has a tendency to be a little overprotective."

"Brian, this is Mrs. Smithers. From now on, she'll be chaperoning you when you surf the Net."

"Here are the keys to the car. And remember, if you get lost, just release the homing pigeons."

Never let your parents chaperone a school dance.

Sing out loud in the car even, or especially,
if it embarrasses your children.

Marilyn Penland

"Are you trying to destroy my social life?
I know people around here, Dad!
Please take off that stupid hat!"

"Oh, look at this! Our little girl coming home from her first date!
You kids just go ahead and say good night
as though we're not even here!"

Lisa's dad had a surefire method for getting her downstairs in time for dates.

Peggy's chances of getting a second date with Jack Mangiante took a turn for the worse when her dad started playing the theme to "Gilligan's Island" on his teeth.

OH, I KNOW! TOTALLY! HE IS SOOOOO CUTE! OOOH! HANG ON, TRISH, I'VE GOT ANOTHER CALL COMING IN! HELLO?
CARLA, THIS IS YOUR FATHER! WILL YOU PLEASE PASS THE POTATOES?!
McPHERSON

As a teenager you are at the last stage in your life when you will be happy to hear that the phone is for you.

Fran Lebowitz

Stella's father should have known better than to try to answer the phone when she was expecting calls from potential prom dates.

Todd's fake cast works like a charm.

Prospective dates first had to give a full presentation to Debbie Wexler's parents.

Anyone who thinks the art of conversation is dead ought to tell a child to go to bed.

Robert Gallagher

"Okay. There are no monsters under your bed! There will never be monsters under your bed again, ever! Now get to sleep."

McPHERSON
THEN AGAIN, IF YOU HAPPENED TO BUY, OH, LET'S SAY 36 BOXES OF GIRL SCOUT COOKIES FROM MY DAUGHTER, I MIGHT CONSIDER RAISING YOUR PERFORMANCE REVIEW FROM "UNSATISFACTORY" TO "SATISFACTORY."
THIN MINTS
THIN MINTS
THIN MINTS

"Tom built a dollhouse for the girls with a full basement."

Whenever one of his daughters returned from a date, Mr. Shelburne would carefully dust her for fingerprints.

The Remleys face that awkward moment in many parents' lives when a teenage daughter brings home a less-than-ideal boyfriend.

Watching your daughter being collected by her date feels like handing over a million-dollar Stradivarius to a gorilla.

Jim Bishop

Before taking her out, Charlene's dates were required to take a brief vocabulary lesson.

As Brad waited for his date,
an excruciating silence fell over the room.

Having passed the state's driver's exam,
Tammy now had to pass her father's grueling twelve-part version.

"Well, too bad, Honey. The only diaper changing station they have is in the women's room. Looks like it's up to you."

"Mike, watch me demonstrate how the force field around my daughter works using this old shoe. Oooo! Look at that. Totally disintegrated."

Any kid will run any errand for you if you ask at bedtime.

Red Skelton

"There! Now you've got no reason to wake us up at three A.M. asking for a glass of water."

You can learn many things from children.
How much patience you have, for instance.

Franklin P. Jones

Determined to get their twenty-five-year-old son, Lanny, out of the house, the Dermsleys make a desperate decision.

Whenever Diane had a new date,
her father liked to play his recordings of guys
who didn't get her home by midnight.

"Once he turns eighteen, he has seven options to pay you back:
(1) five months on a Russian whaler,
(2) six months tending a yak herd in Mongolia . . ."

*There isn't a child who hasn't gone out
into the brave new world who eventually
doesn't return to the old homestead
carrying a bundle of dirty clothes.*

Art Buchwald

The Norstadts devise a subtle plan to force their newly returned adult son to move out.

Human beings are the only creatures on Earth that allow their children to come back home.

Bill Cosby

Overcome by curiosity, the Feeglemans open the door to the Trojan Horse and unwittingly allow their three grown children to move back home.

While rearranging Brandon's room during
his freshman year in college, the Cranstons discover
he'd been telling the truth all these years.

Supporting Others

In the spirit and tradition of the *Chicken Soup for the Soul* series, we designate a charity to receive a portion of the net profits from each book. A portion of the proceeds from this book will be given to **The Horatio Alger Association of Distinguished Americans.**

The Horatio Alger Association of Distinguished Americans has honored the accomplishments and achievements of outstanding individuals in our society who have succeeded in the face of adversity since 1947. The Association encourages young people to pursue their dreams with determination and perseverance by bringing the "Horatio Alger Heroes" of today together with those of tomorrow by bestowing the Horatio Alger Award annually. This award bestows over $5 million in college scholarships and provides an internship and job placement program.

You may contact this organization at:

The Horatio Alger Association
99 Canal Center Plaza
Alexandria, VA 22314
phone: 703-684-9444 • fax: 703-548-3822
Web site: *www.horatioalger.com*

Who Is Jack Canfield?

Jack Canfield is one of America's leading experts in the development of human potential and personal effectiveness. He is both a dynamic, entertaining speaker and a highly sought-after trainer. Jack has a wonderful ability to inform and inspire audiences toward increased levels of self-esteem and peak performance.

He is the author and narrator of several bestselling audio- and videocassette programs, including *Self-Esteem and Peak Performance, How to Build High Self-Esteem, Self-Esteem in the Classroom* and *Chicken Soup for the Soul—Live.* He is regularly seen on television shows such as *Good Morning America, 20/20* and *NBC Nightly News.* Jack has coauthored numerous books, including the *Chicken Soup for the Soul* series, *Dare to Win* and *The Aladdin Factor* (all with Mark Victor Hansen), *100 Ways to Build Self-Concept in the Classroom* (with Harold C. Wells), *Heart at Work* (with Jacqueline Miller) and *The Power of Focus* (with Les Hewitt and Mark Victor Hansen).

For further information about Jack's books, tapes and training programs, or to schedule him for a presentation, please contact:

Jack Canfield
P.O. Box 30880
Santa Barbara, CA 93130
phone: 805-563-2935 • fax: 805-563-2945
Web site: *www.chickensoup.com*

Who Is Mark Victor Hansen?

Mark Victor Hansen is a professional speaker who in the last twenty years has made over 4,000 presentations to more than 2 million people in thirty-two countries. His presentations cover sales excellence and strategies; personal empowerment and development; and how to triple your income and double your time off.

Mark has spent a lifetime dedicated to his mission of making a profound and positive difference in people's lives. Throughout his career, he has inspired hundreds of thousands of people to create a more powerful and purposeful future for themselves while stimulating the sale of billions of dollars worth of goods and services.

Mark is a prolific writer and has authored *Future Diary, How to Achieve Total Prosperity* and *The Miracle of Tithing*. He is coauthor of the *Chicken Soup for the Soul* series, *Dare to Win* and *The Aladdin Factor* (all with Jack Canfield), *The Master Motivator* (with Joe Batten) and *The One Minute Millionaire* with Robert D. Allen.

For further information about Mark, write:

MVH & Associates
P.O. Box 7665
Newport Beach, CA 92658
phone: 949-759-9304 or 800-433-2314
fax: 949-722-6912
Web site: *www.chickensoup.com*

Who Is John McPherson?

John McPherson was raised in a faraway place called Painted Post, New York. (We're not making this up.) He began cartooning at the age of four, with the bulk of his work appearing on walls, furniture and, at one point, a neighbor's dog. Most of this early work was poorly received. Discouraged, John turned his creative efforts to Play-Doh, pipe cleaners and Spirograph.

For the next fifteen years, John put his cartooning career on hold, until one day, during a very dull college engineering class, John drew a doodle in his notebook. His career was reborn. From that point in 1983, John began to draw voraciously despite the fact that his cartoons looked like he had drawn them using a pencil taped to his nose.

In the years that followed, John's cartoons appeared regularly in over forty magazines, and in 1992 Universal Press Syndicate and John teamed up to launch *Close to Home.* Since that time, *Close to Home* has earned its way into 700 papers worldwide, including *The Washington Post, Los Angeles Times, Tokyo Times* and *Hanoi Daily News.* In addition, John has published numerous book collections of his work, a yearly block calendar and an award-winning line of greeting cards with Recycled Paper Products.

In addition to his cartooning, John is an active speaker, talking to groups about the rigors of syndicated cartooning. He can be reached at *closetohome@compuserve.com.*

John lives in Saratoga Springs, New York, with his wife and two boys. When not drawing cartoons or playing with his kids, John spends time expanding his collection of soda-can pull tabs.